## EDGE BOOKS™

# INFECTED!

# BUBONIC PLAGUE

## HOW THE BLACK DEATH CHANGED HISTORY

by Barbara Krasner

**Consultant**

Sharon DeWitte, PhD
Associate Professor of Anthropology
University of South Carolina

**CAPSTONE PRESS**
a capstone imprint

Edge Books are published by Capstone Press,
1710 Roe Crest Drive, North Mankato, Minnesota 56003
www.mycapstone.com

**Library of Congress Cataloging-in-Publication Data**
Names: Krasner, Barbara, author.
Title: Bubonic plague : how the Black Death changed history / by Barbara
   Krasner.
Description: North Mankato, Minnesota : Capstone Press, [2019] | Series:
   Infected! | "Edge Books are published by Capstone Press." | Audience: Ages
   8-14. | Audience: Grades 4 to 6. | Includes bibliographical references and
   index.
Identifiers: LCCN 2018036896 (print) | LCCN 2018038061 (ebook) | ISBN
   9781543555165 (ebook) | ISBN 9781543555073 (hardcover : alk. paper)
Subjects: LCSH: Black Death--Juvenile literature. | Plague--History--Juvenile
   literature. | Plague--Prevention--Juvenile literature. | Diseases and
   history--Juvenile literature.
Classification: LCC RC172 (ebook) | LCC RC172 .K73 2019 (print) | DDC
   616.9/232--dc23
LC record available at https://lccn.loc.gov/2018036896

**Editorial Credits**
Editor: Maddie Spalding
Designer: Craig Hinton
Production Specialist: Ryan Gale

**Quote Sources**
p. 4, J. B. Bury, *History of the Later Roman Empire: From the Death of Theodosius I to the Death of
Justinian*. New York: Dover Publications, 2011; p. 12, Robert S. Gottfried, *The Black Death: Natural and
Human Disaster in Medieval Europe*. New York: The Free Press, 1983

**Photo Credits**
Alamy: David Cole/Press Portrait Service, 9, The Advertising Archives, 24, The History Collection,
20, The Print Collector, 12–13; AP Images: Alexander Joe, 27; iStockphoto: coopder1, 8, D-Keine, 11;
Newscom: akg-images, 15, Everett Collection, 23, World History Archive, 19; Shutterstock Images: Alp
Aksoy, 5, Channarong Pherngjanda, cover (plague doctor), Dudarev Mikhail, 28, Everett Historical, 7,
Hein Nouwens, cover (flea), Kuznetsov Alexey, cover (background), Valery Shanin, 17

**Design Elements**
Shutterstock Images: ilolab

Printed in the United States of America.
PA48

# TABLE OF CONTENTS

# CHAPTER 1

# AN ANCIENT DISEASE

In July AD 541 many people began to die of a strange disease in the Egyptian city of Pelusium. The disease started with fever. **Lymph nodes** on a person's neck, armpits, or thighs became swollen. Purple spots appeared on the person's skin. Some people also had black blisters called pustules. If pustules appeared, the infected person died within a day. The historian Procopius wrote, "Death came in some cases immediately, in others after many days."

This sickness was the bubonic plague. In October it spread through Constantinople. The city of Constantinople was located within the Byzantine Empire in present-day Istanbul, Turkey.

lymph node—a small bean-shaped organ that contains white blood cells, which help fight infections and diseases

About 300,000 people lived in the city. Historians estimate that about 10,000 people died each day. Doctors at the time had never seen this type of disease before. They could not treat the victims.

Today visitors can see the walls of the ancient city of Constantinople in present-day Turkey.

It took about 200 years for the plague to finally die out in the Byzantine Empire. By then towns throughout the empire had emptied. About 25 million people died from the plague. This breakout of the plague was a **pandemic**. It affected many people throughout the empire, which was located along the Mediterranean and Black Seas. Towns and cities were no longer thriving. There were not enough people to build roads, buildings, and other structures. Plans to continue to expand the empire stopped. The armies were simply too small.

No one knew for sure where the plague had come from. This was the first recorded plague pandemic. It was called the Plague of Justinian.

**FAST FACT**

The Plague of Justinian was named after Justinian I, the ruler of the Byzantine Empire.

pandemic—an outbreak of a disease that spreads across several countries or continents and affects many people

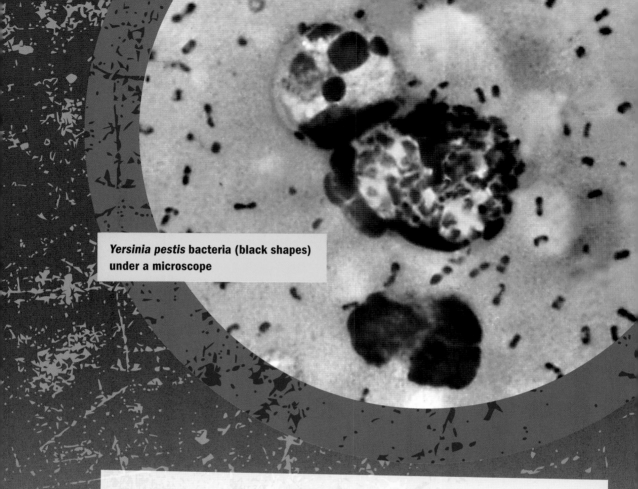

*Yersinia pestis* bacteria (black shapes) under a microscope

## WHAT IS THE BUBONIC PLAGUE?

A certain type of **bacterium** called *Yersinia pestis* causes the bubonic plague. Fleas, lice, and other insects that feed on animal blood carry the bacteria. These insects often live on **rodents** and other animals. The insects bite humans. Then the bacteria get into a person's body.

bacterium—a small living thing that can be found in water, in soil, or in plants and animals
rodent—a small mammal that has sharp front teeth

The bubonic plague affects a person's lymphatic system. This system is a network of lymph nodes and organs that carry fluid throughout the body. The fluid contains white blood cells, which help the body fight infection. Swollen lymph nodes are a sign of infection. The plague bacteria multiply, making it harder for the infected person's body to fight infection. The bubonic plague can kill between 40 and 70 percent of infected people if left untreated.

## TYPES OF THE PLAGUE

If the bubonic plague is not treated, it can lead to worse forms of the plague. The plague bacteria may enter a person's bloodstream and cause septicemic plague. This type of plague can cause a person's skin tissue to die. Victims have fevers, chills, and stomach pain. The bacteria can also infect a person's lungs. This type of plague is called pneumonic plague.

Pneumonic plague is the deadliest form of the plague. It is the only type of plague that can be **transmitted** directly from person to person. Infected people can spread the disease to others when they cough or sneeze. Victims have fevers, chest pain, and trouble breathing.

Septicemic plague can cause a person's skin tissue to die and turn black.

transmit—to pass on something from one living thing to another

# CHAPTER 2

# THE BLACK DEATH

The Plague of Justinian died out in about
AD 750. The next plague pandemic hit Europe in
the mid-1300s. Outbreaks started in Constantinople
and Messina, Italy. These were both large coastal
cities. Ships carried goods to and from these cities.
Some people think flea-infected rats came aboard
the ships. As the ships traveled, so did the plague.
But some historians think the plague spread in
a different way. Because the disease spread so
quickly, they think it was transmitted from person
to person through the air. They think the disease
might have been the pneumonic plague.

The plague quickly spread to North Africa, Spain, England, and Scandinavia. Then it spread to Poland and Russia. The plague affected everyday life. Wars and trade stopped.

## THE CAPTURE OF CAFFA

In 1346 Mongolian people from Central Asia wanted to capture the city of Caffa by the Black Sea. Some of the Mongolians had died from the plague. The Mongolians hurled the dead bodies over the city walls. The plague spread to the city's residents. Most historians believe the infected dead bodies caused this plague outbreak. Many people in the city died. This allowed the Mongolian people to easily take over the city.

When disease-infected rats travel on ships, they can spread disease between distant locations.

No one could figure out what exactly caused the plague. Some people thought bad-smelling air spread the disease. Others blamed people for the plague. Many Roman Catholics blamed Jewish people. In Germany, France, and Belgium, thousands of Jewish people were killed.

Historians estimate that the plague killed as many as 50 million people between 1346 and 1353. One historian at the time wrote, "So many died that all believed it was the end of the world." This sickness later became known as the Black Death. It was named after the dark spots that appeared on a victim's skin. The Black Death came to an end in 1353. But plague **epidemics** happened occasionally in Europe. These outbreaks affected people within the region. The last major plague epidemic in England happened in 1665 and 1666. It was called the Great Plague of London. One writer recorded 10,000 deaths in the city within one week. More than 68,500 people died during this epidemic.

epidemic—an outbreak of a disease that affects many people within a particular region

The last major plague epidemic in Western Europe happened in 1720. It spread through France. More than 39,000 people died. The plague then hit Moscow, Russia, in late 1770. Some historians estimate that about 200,000 people died from this epidemic.

The bodies of plague victims were put on carts and taken outside of London to be buried.

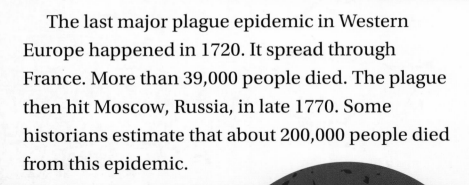

**FAST FACT**

Doctors tried many treatments to cure the plague. One English doctor strapped a live chicken to a patient's swollen lymph nodes. He thought the sickness would spread to the chicken and heal the patient.

# CHAPTER 3

# STUDYING THE PLAGUE

The Black Death was not the last plague pandemic. In 1855 the bubonic plague emerged in southwestern China. Tens of thousands of people died in China alone. By the late 1800s the plague had spread to the Chinese cities of Hong Kong and Guangzhou. Traders from China traveled to other parts of the world on ships. Infected rats on board the ships spread the plague from China to many other parts of the world. Fleas on infected rats later moved to squirrels and other small mammals. In this way, the plague spread to parts of North and South America. It also spread throughout Asia, Australia, Africa, and Europe. This pandemic was called the Modern Plague.

## PLAGUE DOCTORS

From the 1600s through the 1800s, plague doctors tried to treat people with the plague. Towns or villages hired a plague doctor when an outbreak occurred. Plague doctors wore masks with a long nose like a beak. They thought bad-smelling air spread the plague from person to person. They put dried flowers, herbs, and spices inside the masks to keep from smelling this bad air. To prevent contact with patients, they wore gloves and long robes that covered their entire bodies. They commonly treated patients by bloodletting. This process involved draining a patient's blood.

Plague doctors often carried canes to examine patients without touching them.

Before the 1800s many people thought bad-smelling air spread the plague. But French scientist Louis Pasteur had a different idea. Pasteur believed **germs** spread the plague. Swiss doctor Alexandre Yersin worked for Pasteur and the French Medical Corps. Yersin went to Hong Kong in 1894 to study the plague.

In Hong Kong Yersin injected guinea pigs with fluid taken from a dead victim's swollen lymph node. The guinea pigs died. Yersin found rod-shaped bacteria in the guinea pigs. This was the same type of bacteria he had found in infected people.

Hong Kong's streets were filled with dead rats. Yersin studied these rats. He also found rod-shaped bacteria in the rats. He found that both rats and people died from the same bacterium. This discovery led scientists to believe that the plague spread from rats to humans.

**germ**—something that causes disease, such as a bacterium or virus

Yersin created a **serum** from the plague bacterium in 1896. A serum is a fluid that contains a small dose of a disease. It is injected into a healthy person. It helps a person's body learn how to fight infection.

BAC SI
ALEXANDRE YERSIN
(1863 - 1943)

A memorial in Vietnam honors Alexandre Yersin for his medical discoveries.

serum—a fluid containing a small dose of a disease that helps a person's body learn how to fight an infection

Yersin's serum was first used in 1896 when a plague outbreak occurred in Bombay, India. In 1897 the *Indian Medical Gazette* reported that the serum got rid of plague **symptoms** in 24 of 26 cases. These patients recovered from the plague.

Russian scientist Waldemar Haffkine traveled to Bombay during the 1896 outbreak. He came up with another way to fight the plague. He experimented on rabbits. He killed a sample of plague bacteria. He injected the dead bacteria into the rabbits. He later injected them with live plague bacteria. But the rabbits did not get the plague. The **vaccine** had protected them from the disease. Their bodies had developed ways to fight the bacteria.

## FAST FACT

In 1897 Waldemar Haffkine injected himself with his plague vaccine to test it. He did not get the plague.

**symptom**—a change in a person's body or mind that is a sign of a disease
**vaccine**—a substance made up of dead, weakened, or living organisms that is injected into a person to protect against a disease

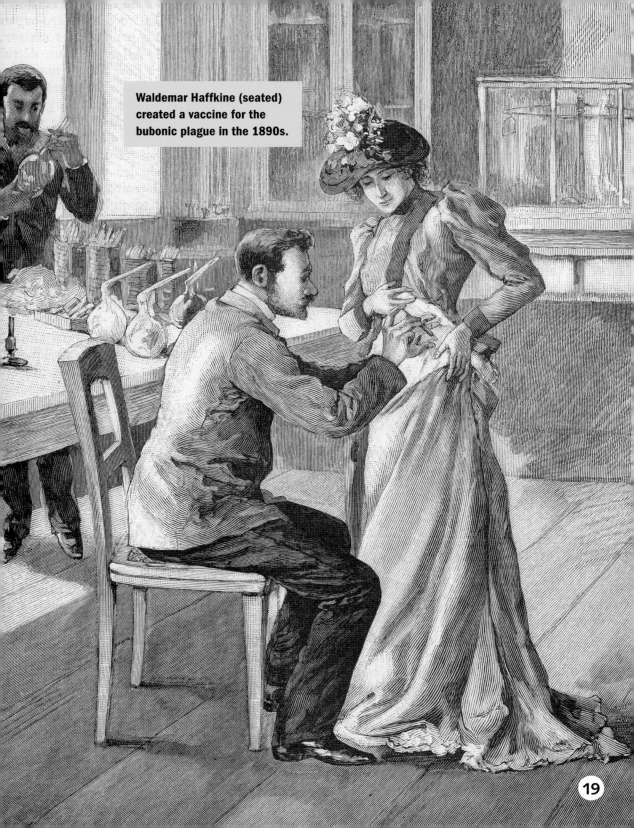

Waldemar Haffkine (seated) created a vaccine for the bubonic plague in the 1890s.

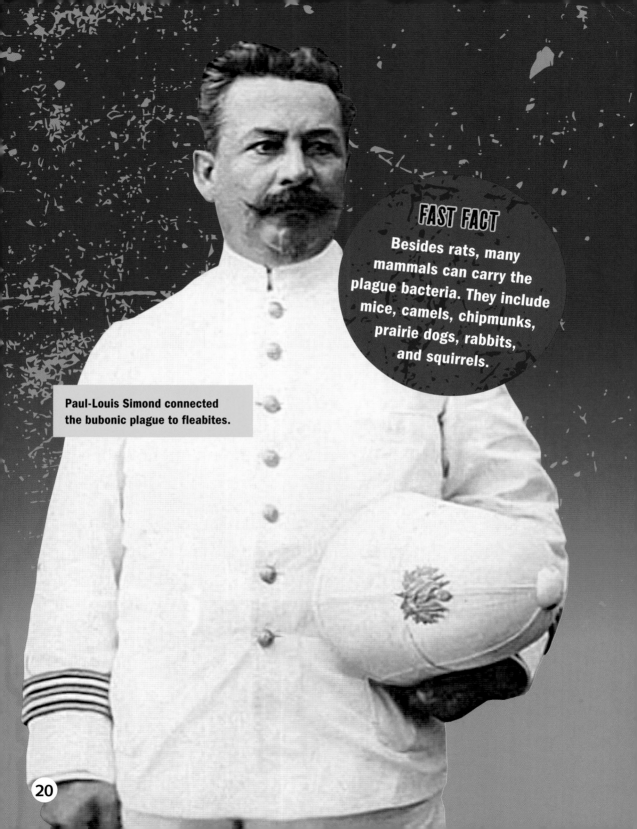

Paul-Louis Simond connected the bubonic plague to fleabites.

Haffkine's vaccine was later used on volunteers at a prison in Bombay when a plague outbreak struck. Only three of the 154 volunteers got the plague. The vaccine was later tested throughout India. It protected many people against the bubonic plague. But it did not protect against the deadlier septicemic or pneumonic plagues.

## LATER DISCOVERIES

Researchers could not agree on how the plague spread. French doctor Paul-Louis Simond also worked with Pasteur. He traveled to southern Vietnam in 1898 when the region was struck by an outbreak. Simond wanted to find out how the plague spread from rats to humans.

Simond experimented with rats. He placed an infected rat that did not have fleas in a container with a healthy rat. The healthy rat stayed healthy until Simond put fleas in the container. Then the healthy rat became infected. It died from the plague. Simond discovered that bites from infected fleas cause the plague to spread.

# FIGHTING THE PLAGUE

Throughout the 1900s scientists continued to find new ways to fight the plague. In 1937 scientists created drugs called sulphonamides. These drugs fought bacterial infections. They helped prevent people from getting the bubonic plague. They were cheap and widely available.

Even more powerful drugs known as antibiotics were made in 1946. Doctors injected these drugs into a person's body. The drugs killed harmful bacteria or kept the bacteria from multiplying. One antibiotic called streptomycin was created to treat the disease tuberculosis. Scientists discovered that it could also be used to treat the bubonic plague.

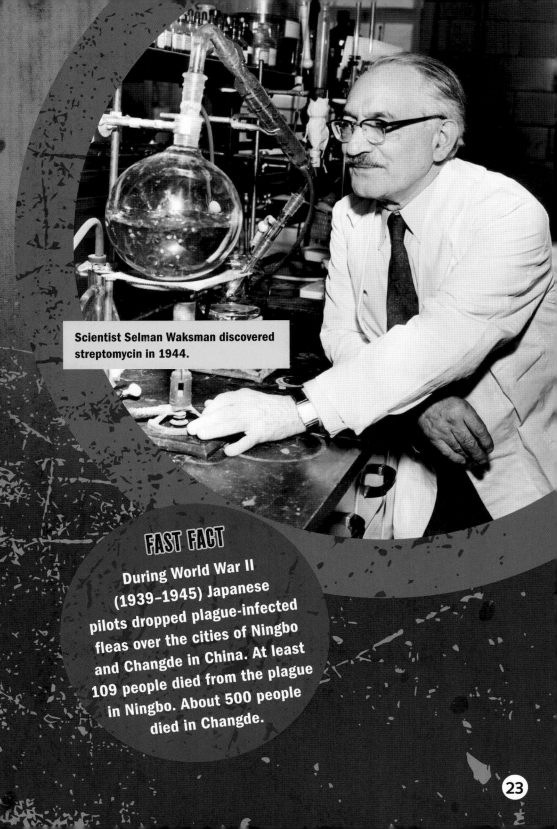

Scientist Selman Waksman discovered streptomycin in 1944.

## FAST FACT

During World War II (1939–1945) Japanese pilots dropped plague-infected fleas over the cities of Ningbo and Changde in China. At least 109 people died from the plague in Ningbo. About 500 people died in Changde.

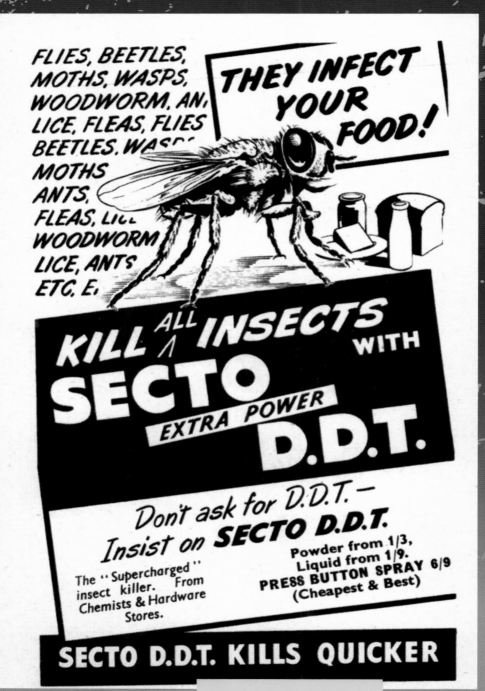

A 1950s poster advertised the insect-killing power of DDT.

Scientists also explored ways to keep the plague from spreading. They developed chemicals that could kill infected fleas. Scientists discovered that a chemical called DDT could kill insects. Soldiers sprayed DDT to kill disease-carrying insects during World War II. But health authorities noticed that DDT harmed people and the environment. DDT was banned in the United States in 1972.

Scientists found other ways to fight the spread of the plague after DDT was banned. They discovered that dusting rodent burrows with certain chemicals can kill fleas. They found that insect repellant sprays can help keep fleas from biting people. These methods helped bring down the number of bubonic plague cases.

**FAST FACT**
People also used DDT to kill lice that caused typhus and mosquitoes that caused malaria.

# CHAPTER 5

# A BRIGHTER FUTURE

Antibiotics have helped scientists fight the bubonic plague. But there are still occasional cases in North and South America, Africa, and Asia. From 2010 to 2015, countries around the world reported 3,248 cases of the plague and 584 plague-related deaths. The countries that are most affected include the Democratic Republic of the Congo, Madagascar, and Peru. Sometimes people in these countries do not have access to swift medical treatment.

**FAST FACT**

In 2017 a plague epidemic killed 202 people in Madagascar.

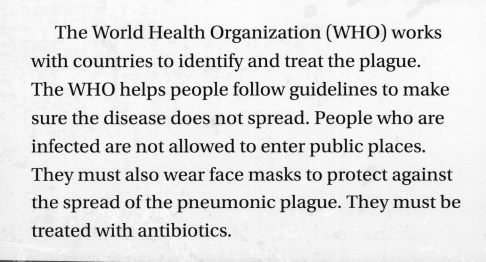

The World Health Organization (WHO) works with countries to identify and treat the plague. The WHO helps people follow guidelines to make sure the disease does not spread. People who are infected are not allowed to enter public places. They must also wear face masks to protect against the spread of the pneumonic plague. They must be treated with antibiotics.

**Red Cross volunteers educate people in Madagascar about the plague in 2017.**

Madagascar's capital city, Antananarivo, was hit by a plague epidemic in 2017.

## THE PLAGUE TODAY

In Madagascar plague outbreaks happen every year. Scientists discovered new **strains** of the plague in Madagascar in 1995 and 1996. The drugs available then could not fight against these new forms of plague bacteria. In 2017 new antibiotics were developed. These drugs show promise. Scientists continue to test them.

Today there are only about seven cases of the plague in the United States each year. Most cases of the bubonic plague are easily treated. Antibiotics have reduced the death rate from the plague to 11 percent in the United States.

Scientists and health care workers are hopeful that they can continue to reduce the number of plague cases worldwide. Scientists are working to develop better drugs and vaccines. Health care workers help manage outbreaks. Their work continues to save many lives.

strain—a variety or subtype of a living thing, such as a bacterium

# GLOSSARY

**bacterium** (bak-TEER-ee-uhm)—a small living thing that can be found in water, in soil, or in plants and animals

**epidemic** (eh-pih-DEH-mik)—an outbreak of a disease that affects many people within a particular region

**germ** (JURM)—something that causes disease, such as a bacterium or virus

**lymph node** (LIMF NOHD)—a small bean-shaped organ that contains white blood cells, which help fight infections and diseases

**pandemic** (pan-DEH-mik)—an outbreak of a disease that spreads across several countries or continents and affects many people

**rodent** (ROH-dint)—a small mammal that has sharp front teeth

**serum** (SEER-uhm)—a fluid containing a small dose of a disease that helps a person's body learn how to fight an infection

**strain** (STRAYN)—a variety or subtype of a living thing, such as a bacterium

**symptom** (SIM-tuhm)—a change in a person's body or mind that is a sign of a disease

**transmit** (tranz-MIT)—to pass on something from one living thing to another

**vaccine** (vak-SEEN)—a substance made up of dead, weakened, or living organisms that is injected into a person to protect against a disease

# READ MORE

Henry, Claire. *The World's Deadliest Epidemics*. The World's Deadliest. New York: PowerKids Press, 2014.

Levy, Janey. *Plague: The Black Death*. Doomed! New York: Gareth Stevens Publishing, 2016.

Throp, Claire. *The Horror of the Bubonic Plague*. Deadly History. North Mankato, Minn.: Capstone Press, 2018.

# INTERNET SITES

Use FactHound to find Internet sites related to this book.

Visit www.facthound.com

Just type in 9781543555073 and go.

Super-cool stuff!

Check out projects, games and lots more at
**www.capstonekids.com**

# INDEX